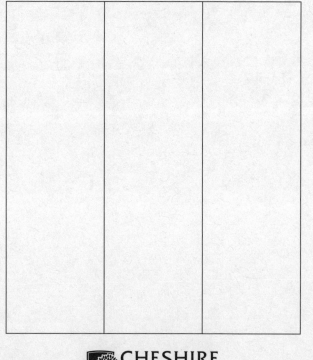

TECHNOLOGY AT WORK

# AT THE
# FACTORY

**Louise Spilsbury**

Raintree

## www.raintreepublishers.co.uk

Visit our website to find out more information about Raintree books.

To order:

☎ Phone 44 (0) 1865 888112

🖹 Send a fax to 44 (0) 1865 314091

💻 Visit the Raintree bookshop at www.raintreepublishers.co.uk to browse our catalogue and order online.

Raintree is an imprint of Pearson Education Limited, a company incorporated in England and Wales having its registered office at Edinburgh Gate, Harlow, Essex, CM20 2JE – Registered company number: 00872828

Raintree is a registered trademark of Pearson Education Ltd.

Edited by Louise Galpine and Rachel Howells
Designed by Richard Parker and Tinstar Design Ltd
Original illustrations© Pearson Education Ltd
Illustrations by Darren Lingard
Picture Research by Hannah Taylor and Catherine Bevan
Originated by Modern Age
Printed and bound in China by CTPS

13-digit ISBN  978 1 4062 0985 3
13 12 11 10 09
10 9 8 7 6 5 4 3 2 1

### British Library Cataloguing in Publication Data
Spilsbury, Louise
    At the factory. - (Technology at work)
     670
A full catalogue record for this book is available from the British Library.

### Acknowledgements
The publishers would like to thank the following for permission to reproduce photographs: ©A1 Pix p. 9; ©Alamy pp. 4 (Simon Clay), 5 (Adrian Sherratt), 7 (Trip), 10 (vario images GmbH & Co.KG), 11 (I.Glory), 28 bottom left (vario images GmbH & Co.KG), 15 (ImageState), 18 (eStock), 27 (Justin Kase zonez); ©Corbis pp. 8, 28 top right (Tim Wright), 24 (TWPhoto), 25 (Kevin Fleming); ©Getty Images pp. 6 (Stone/ Michael Rosenfeld), 19 (Johannes Simon), 28 top left (Stone/ Michael Rosenfeld), 19 (Johannes Simon); ©istockphoto/ VisualField p. 29 left; ©Wishlist Images p. 29 right.

Cover photograph of robotic welder, reproduced with permission of ©Getty Images (Photographer's Choice).

Every effort has been made to contact copyright holders of any material reproduced in this book. Any omissions will be rectified in subsequent printings if notice is given to the publishers.

We would like to thank Ian Graham for his invaluable help in the preparation of this book.

# CONTENTS

Inside a factory ........................................................ 4

Designing a car........................................................ 6

Testing the design .................................................... 8

Making a car body .................................................. 10

Putting the pieces together ...................................... 12

Automatic machines ................................................ 14

How a robot arm works ............................................ 16

Painting a car.......................................................... 18

Vital parts .............................................................. 20

Car power!.............................................................. 22

Completing a car .................................................... 24

Delivering cars........................................................ 26

Factory technology .................................................. 28

Glossary.................................................................. 30

Find out more ........................................................ 31

Index ...................................................................... 32

Some words are printed in bold, **like this**. You can find out what they mean by looking in the glossary.

# INSIDE A FACTORY

A factory is a building where workers make things to sell. In most factories workers have different jobs but they all help to make the same thing. For example, in a car factory some people make the body of a car and others fit the seats inside. Workers use **machines** to help them work faster and for a longer time without getting tired.

In this factory, cars are made on **assembly lines**. Cars sit on moving platforms that carry them to different machines or people that add different parts.

AT WORK

## PIECES IN A PUZZLE

A car is made from as many as 9,000 individual parts.
It takes between 5 and 30 hours to put the parts together in the factory!

## What is a machine?

A machine is a device that makes a **force** greater. Forces are pushes or pulls. For example, you use a knife to eat with because pushing down on the blade makes it easier to slice food into pieces. Using machines means we can do more work with less **effort**. In factories workers often use **forklift** trucks to lift weights or loads. They push spikes underneath the load and press a button that raises the spikes. Workers using a forklift truck can carry heavy loads all day long.

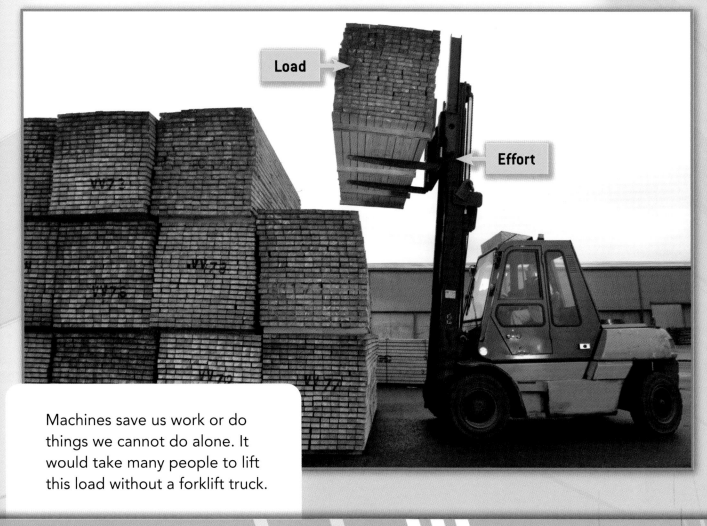

Load

Effort

Machines save us work or do things we cannot do alone. It would take many people to lift this load without a forklift truck.

# DESIGNING A CAR

The first stage in making any new product is the **design**. Car designers think about who will use the car, for example a family car needs more seats and space inside than a sports car. They consider the size, the shape of the car body, the layout of the inside, the colour, and materials to use for seats. Then the designers make sketches using their ideas.

Using a computer makes it easy to change things like the colour, shape, and size of different parts of a design without having to draw the whole car again.

AT WORK

## A SLOW PROCESS

Agreeing on the design of a new car can take at least one and a half years! Only then are the new cars made in factories.

## Computer modelling and 3D

Designers use computers to make **three-dimensional** (3D) pictures of their design. This is called computer-aided design, or CAD. They draw designs on a **digital tablet**. The tablet senses the push of a pen against it. What designers draw on the digital tablet instantly appears on the computer screen. By using CAD **programs**, designers can turn the car on screen so people can look at it from every angle.

Sometimes designers make scale models. These are models of the final car but much smaller. This scale model is a quarter the size of the actual car!

## Clay models

Looking at a 3D image of a car on a screen is useful, but often the best way to spot design problems is to make a model. Design models must be accurate. Some car models are made by hand from foam and are then covered in clay. Others are made by **machines** that follow the CAD design of the car to produce the model.

# TESTING THE DESIGN

To find out if a new **design** works properly, designers create a **prototype**. A prototype is a bit like a real car, with working parts that operate properly. However, it is made slowly by hand and not in a factory.

In a crash test the strength and safety of a new car design for its passengers is tested to the limit!

## Safety first

A car prototype goes through different tests to make sure it is strong and safe. In a crash test, workers strap life-size dummies into a car and the car is pushed into a test wall. Testers film the test and take measurements to see how well the car protects passengers inside when it crashes. The car design may be adjusted if the tests do not go well.

# Wind tunnels

Workers also test a prototype by putting it in a **wind tunnel**. This is a room with a giant fan that blows wind fast at the prototype. The smoother the car, the more easily the air can move around it, and the faster the car can travel. After these tests workers may adjust the prototype's shape so air flows more easily past it.

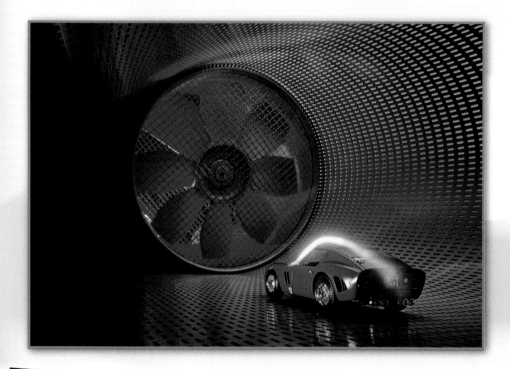

Why do engineers test cars in a wind tunnel like this?

## AT WORK

### USING LESS FUEL

Wind tunnel tests are important because the harder a car works to drive through air, the more fuel its engine uses. One reason that people want cars that use less fuel is because fuel (petrol) is expensive.

# MAKING A CAR BODY

The car body supports the weight of the car and protects the people travelling inside. It is made from pieces of a tough, strong metal called steel. The steel is delivered by lorry to the car factory in giant rolls. The rolls are flattened, cut, and pressed into pieces of the right size and shape to use in a car.

Each roll of steel is the weight of 100 motorbikes.

# Cutting steel

Imagine how hard it would be to cut a steel sheet with scissors or bend it by hand into shapes. Workers use **machines** the size of a house to do the work with less **effort**. First, blades cut the flat shapes of the underneath, front end, sides, roof, and doors of the car from steel. Then the shapes are pressed hard to bend them into the finished pieces.

In the factory, steel is pressed so that it begins to take the shape of the car.

## WEDGE

The blade for cutting steel is a strong, sharp **wedge** shape. A wedge is a simple machine. The sharp edge crushes and splits a gap in the metal. Pressing the thin end of the edge in the narrow gap makes the wedge press against the gap, forcing it to open.

# PUTTING THE PIECES TOGETHER

The car body pieces are joined together by **welding**. This is when two pieces of metal are heated until they melt together. When the metal cools and hardens you cannot see where they join. To melt steel, electricity heats metal devices called electrodes. These weld metal parts together at particular spots. That is why this process is called spot welding.

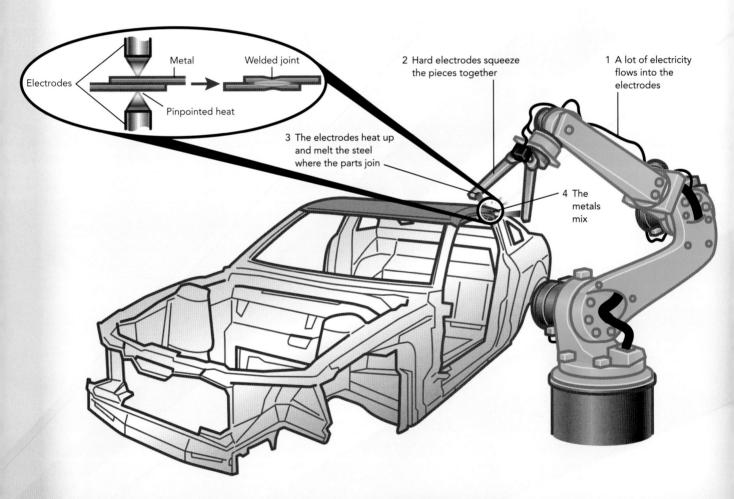

Electrodes

Metal

Welded joint

Pinpointed heat

2 Hard electrodes squeeze the pieces together

1 A lot of electricity flows into the electrodes

3 The electrodes heat up and melt the steel where the parts join

4 The metals mix

# ELECTRICITY INTO HEAT

Electrodes heat up because of high resistance. This is when electricity cannot move easily through a material. Electricity is produced by the movement of tiny, invisible particles called electrons. We can think of the electrons in the electrode like lots of marathon runners moving along a street into a narrow alley. They bunch up, jogging around and getting hot!

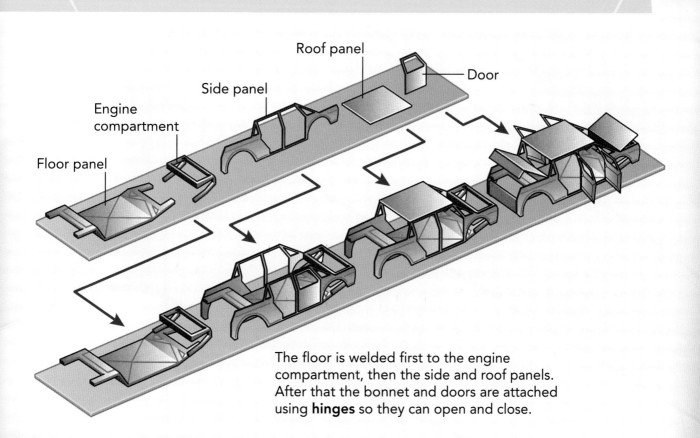

Roof panel

Door

Side panel

Engine
compartment

Floor panel

The floor is welded first to the engine compartment, then the side and roof panels. After that the bonnet and doors are attached using **hinges** so they can open and close.

# AUTOMATIC MACHINES

In many factories a lot of the heavy and simple work happens automatically without people. For example, **conveyor belts** move complete car bodies through the factory. A conveyor belt is a belt made of flexible rubber or hard metal plates **hinged** together. A motor makes the belt move along over rollers, carrying whatever is on top smoothly along. Sometimes cars rest on stilts on the conveyor belt or on wheeled trolleys on tracks.

## Machine workers

**Robots** are **machines** that automatically do particular jobs. In a car factory, robots **weld**, paint, and lift weights. Factory workers **program** the robots to complete a job.

Robots have some advantages over people as workers. They never get tired, they do exactly the same job each time, they do not need to be paid, and they can do unsafe or dirty work without getting hurt. However, robots are expensive and can only do what they are programmed to do.

### IN THE FUTURE

Robots could program teams of other robots in factories and even drive cars!

Most of the welding in a car factory is done by robots! Here you can see the tracks of the conveyor belt that the car bodies move along on.

# HOW A ROBOT ARM WORKS

The **robots** in a car factory are really robot arms! Just like our arms, a robot arm is made of different parts that move at joints. However, the parts move using the power of motors rather than muscles.

1. Workers **program** a computer to control how the arm moves.

2. Each joint is powered by an electric motor allowing parts of the arm to rotate towards or away from each other by small amounts.

3. The last part of the arm is the bit that carries out the task of the robot arm, such as welding or lifting. It has a **sensor** on it to help it do the job properly and for people to check up on how well it has been programmed to do the job.

**AT WORK**

## SENSING A ROBOT'S WORK

Sensors are special electronic devices that measure a robot's work and movement. For example, some sensors can tell how tightly a robot hand is gripping and others can tell the distance from another object. This means robot arms can do their job automatically, exactly the same way each time, without being stopped and started by workers.

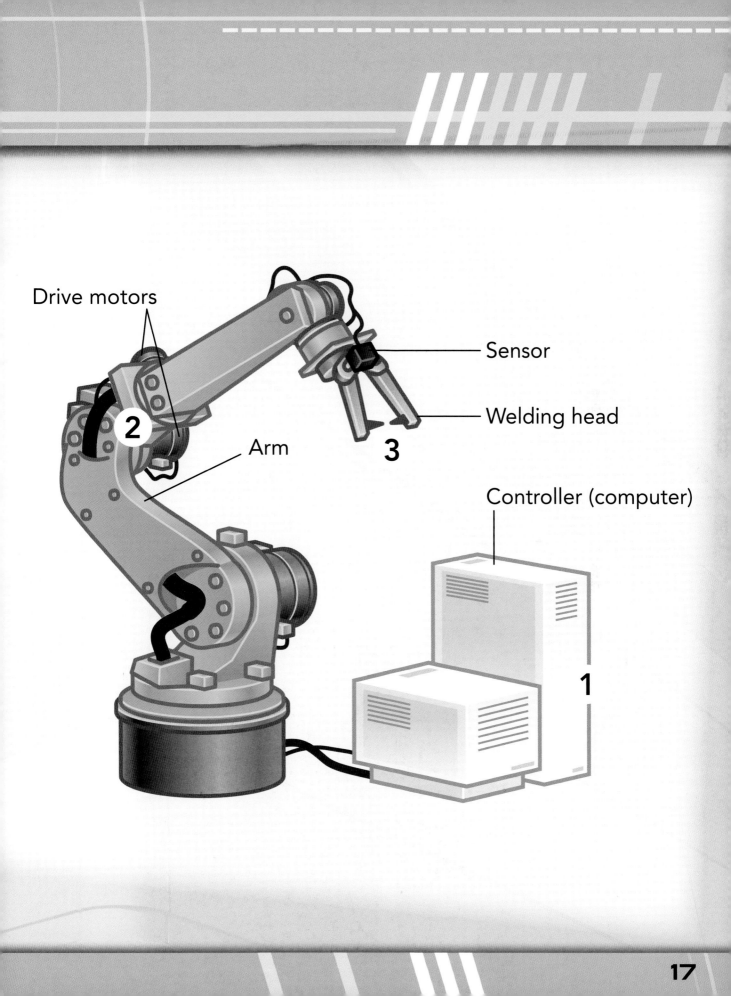

Drive motors

Sensor

Welding head

Arm

Controller (computer)

2

3

1

# PAINTING A CAR

The next stage in making a car is painting the body. The unpainted body moves along the **conveyor belt** into the paint shop in the factory. Before being painted, the car is cleaned up. It is dipped in chemicals and sprayed with water to remove any dirt and oil. Then the wet body is blown dry!

Paint is sprayed on using long hoses that are connected to paint storage tanks.

## FAST FACT

Workers in the paint room wear clothes without any loose fibres so they cannot fall off and stick to the wet paint!

## Three coats

The car body is painted three times. First it moves into a tank of special paint to stop the steel **rusting**. When steel rusts it turns reddish brown and crumbles. This makes a car weak and unsafe. It also looks ugly. The car then moves into an oven that bakes this special paint so it goes hard.

Robot arms like these transform a dull-looking car into a shiny new model.

Next the car moves past spinning sprayers or **robot** arms fitted with sprayer ends that cover the body evenly with paint. A layer of thick grey paint makes the car surface smooth. The last layer is the final colour of the car. Once all the paint is dry, workers glue on pieces that go on the outside of a car, such as the car maker's badge.

# VITAL PARTS

A painted car body may look like a car, but is not yet a proper **vehicle**! All vehicles can move in order to carry loads such as passengers and their luggage. The vital parts that make a car move, such as its engine, are grouped together in the **drive train**. Workers raise the body above the **conveyor belt** so they can connect the drive train from underneath.

## Parts of the drive train

The engine makes power to turn the wheels and drive the car along. The steering system and brakes allow the driver to control the direction and speed the car goes. Giant springs between the wheels and the car body provide **suspension**. The springs absorb jolts when the car drives over bumps, so that passengers have a comfortable ride.

**AT WORK**

### STEERING WHEELS

Car steering works by **rack and pinion**. This **machine** changes turning movements into straight movements. The driver turns the large steering wheel. This then turns the narrow steering shaft that twists the pinion. The pinion is a small cog or wheel with grooves or teeth in it. The teeth on the pinion move against teeth on a bar called the rack. Then the rack moves right or left.

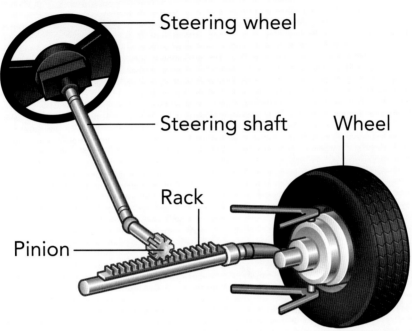

Steering wheel

Steering shaft

Wheel

Rack

Pinion

**Turning left**

Turning the steering wheel slides the rack to one side. It pulls the back of the wheel, which turns outwards and makes the car turn left.

**Turning right**

Turning the steering wheel the other way slides the rack to the other side. It pushes against the back of the wheel, which turns inwards and makes the car turn right.

# CAR POWER!

A car engine is **designed** to produce power. It looks complicated but is actually a fairly simple **machine**. Most car engines are basically a set of four or eight **cylinders** made of very strong metal. Each cylinder is sealed shut with a sliding plunger called a **piston**. There are openings at the top of each cylinder called valves that can open or close. Fuel burns in the cylinders causing explosions that push out the pistons.

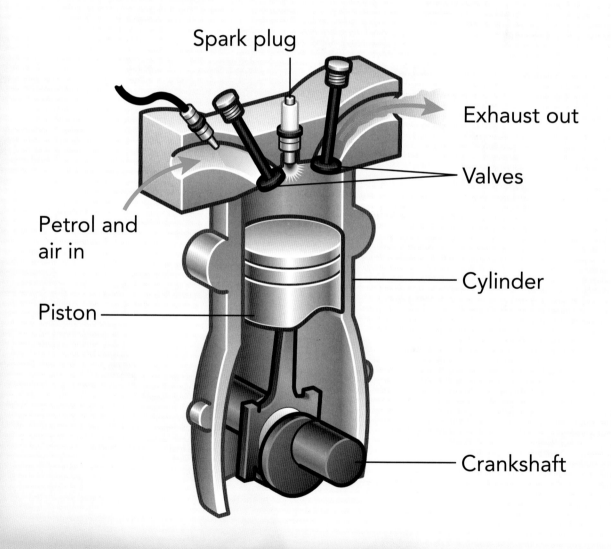

Spark plug

Exhaust out

Valves

Petrol and air in

Cylinder

Piston

Crankshaft

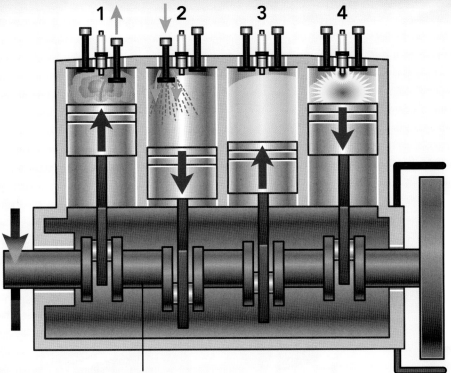

1     2     3     4

Crankshaft

Each piston pushes
out in sequence so
the crankshaft is
spinning the
wheels all the time.

The pistons are attached to an **axle** called a
**crankshaft** that turns the car's wheels when
the pistons push down.

- Petrol and air enter the cylinder.

- The spark plug makes a spark that sets fire
  to the petrol and air.

- Gases made by the fire push the piston down.

- The piston makes the crankshaft rotate.

- Waste gases leave the cylinder and go into
  the exhaust pipe.

## IN THE FUTURE

Cars will soon be able to
use hydrogen gas as fuel.
Hydrogen burns with
oxygen, releasing power
and steam instead of dirty
exhaust gases.

# COMPLETING A CAR

Workers complete a car by adding the final parts. These include the windscreen, bumpers, windscreen wipers, headlights, and the instrument panel. This plastic panel at the front of a car has instruments to control the car such as light switches and the speedometer, which shows how fast a car is moving. Workers make the car comfortable by adding parts such as carpets and music players.

This worker is fitting the car's instrument panel. An instrument panel is also sometimes called a dashboard.

## AT WORK

### IN A SPIN

Workers test drive cars to see they move and can be controlled as they were **designed** to. They drive either on a special track by the factory or by driving over rollers. The spinning tyres make the rollers spin the opposite direction at the same speed. The car stays where it is.

## Testing

The final stage is to test the completed car. Workers switch the car on and connect it to a computer. The computer screen shows information from **sensors** in all the electrical parts, such as the lights and brakes. Workers check the information to make sure everything is working properly.

These shiny new cars are complete and ready to leave the factory.

# DELIVERING CARS

Workers do not drive finished cars from the factory to the shops that sell them. Instead, other **vehicles** transport the cars. Some cars are put onto open carriages of trains that stop near the factory. But most cars are put on lorries called **car transporters**.

1. Many wheels move the transporter on several **axles**. Wheels connected to axles are simple **machines**. The powerful force of the engine turns the narrow axle a short distance. This makes the wheel turn with less force, but over the **circumference** of the wide wheel.

2. The wheels are wide, so the load of cars is supported on the ground by the large area of each tyre.

3. Several ramps can be raised or lowered to let cars onto higher levels or to stack cars together so the transporter can carry more at the same time!

AT WORK

## LETTING LIQUID DO THE WORK

The machines that move the ramps cars drive onto transporters are called **hydraulic** rams. These are shaped rather like **cylinders** with **pistons**. Pumps move liquid in or out of cylinders through long narrow pipes. The liquid moves the wide pistons out a short distance with more **force**.

The heavy load of a car transporter is supported by wide wheels, which give support on the ground.

# FACTORY TECHNOLOGY

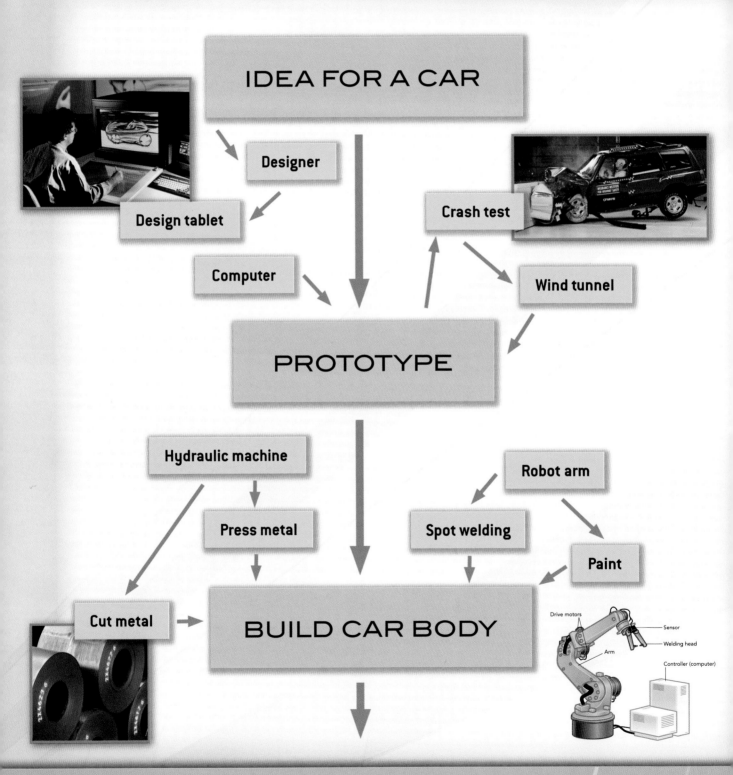

**IDEA FOR A CAR**

Designer

Design tablet

Computer

Crash test

Wind tunnel

**PROTOTYPE**

Hydraulic machine

Press metal

Robot arm

Spot welding

Paint

Cut metal

**BUILD CAR BODY**

Drive motors

Sensor

Welding head

Arm

Controller (computer)

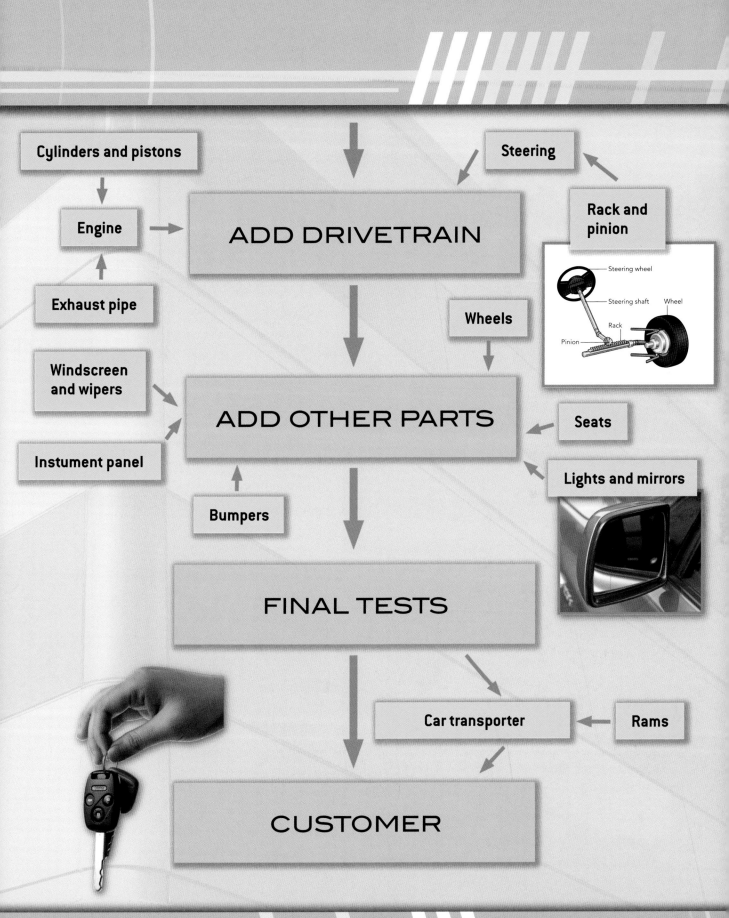

Cylinders and pistons

Engine

Exhaust pipe

ADD DRIVETRAIN

Steering

Rack and pinion

Steering wheel
Steering shaft
Wheel
Rack
Pinion

Wheels

Windscreen and wipers

Instument panel

ADD OTHER PARTS

Seats

Lights and mirrors

Bumpers

FINAL TESTS

Car transporter

Rams

CUSTOMER

# GLOSSARY

**assembly line** system in factories where items being made move between different workers or machines that put together different parts

**axle** shaft or rod on which a wheel turns

**car transporter** long truck to carry cars on

**circumference** distance round a circle

**conveyor belt** moving belt that transports objects. A conveyor belt moves cars through a car factory.

**crankshaft** rotating shaft in the engine turned by the up-and-down movement of the pistons

**cylinder** part in an engine where fuel burns to power a car's wheels

**design** develop a plan for an object, such as a car

**digital tablet** device a car designer draws on to create an image on a computer

**drive train** parts that make a car move. For example, the engine rotates the axle and the steering wheel turns the wheels.

**effort** amount of work needed to complete a task. People use less effort lifting with the help of cranes.

**force** push or pull making something move

**forklift** small vehicle used to lift and move loads over short distances

**hinge** joint that connects two solid objects like a door and a frame. Hinges allow one to swing or move relative to the other.

**hydraulic** moved using liquid

**machine** device that helps us do work. A robot arm is a common machine in car factories.

**piston** piece of metal that moves up and down in a cylinder to help turn the crankshaft

**program** sequence of instructions that computers use to do work. Workers program computers that make robots move and complete a job, such as painting a car.

**prototype** full-scale working model of a new product, such as a car

**rack and pinion** set of gears used to change turning force into a straight motion, to steer cars

**robot** machine that automatically does routine jobs, for example in a factory. People tell robots what to do using computer programs.

**rust** turn red-brown when steel reacts with oxygen in the presence of water. If cars rust they may get weak and unsafe to drive.

**sensor** device that produces an electronic signal when it senses light, distance, or other information

**suspension** how a vehicle is supported on its wheels. Cars are supported by springs.

**three-dimensional** something with depth. People can make things look three-dimensional in drawings using shading and shapes.

**vehicle** machine that carries people or objects. Many vehicles, such as cars, have engines to make them move.

**wedge** triangular-shaped machine that can be used to split open or cut things

**welding** join together by heating and melting

**wind tunnel** room with large fan to blow air over a car or other object

# FIND OUT MORE

## Books

*Car (Eyewitness Books)*, Richard Sutton and Laura Buller
(Dorling Kindersley, 2005)

*Cars (High Interest Books)*, Philip Abraham (Children's Press, 2004)

*The Science of Forces: Projects with Experiments on Forces and
Machines (Tabletop Scientist)*, Steve Parker (Heinemann, 2005)

*What Do Ramps and Wedges Do? (What Do Simple Machines Do?)*,
David Glover (Heinemann Library, 2007)

## Websites

**www.toyota.co.jp/en/kids/car/index.html**

Loads of information about how Toyota cars are made with good
pictures of the process and inside the factory.

**www.explainthatstuff.com/carengines.html**

Try this website if you want more details about how car engines work.

**http://teacher.scholastic.com/dirtrep/simple/index.htm**

Visit this website to learn more about simple machines.

# INDEX

assembly lines 4
axles 23, 26

brakes 20, 25

CAD (computer-aided design) 7
car factories 4, 10-25, 28-29
car transporters 26-27, 29
cars
    brakes 20, 25
    car body 10-11, 28
    car parts 4
    design 6-9, 28
    drive train 20, 29
    engine 20, 22-23, 29
    painting 14, 18-19, 28
    steering system 20, 21, 29
    testing 8-9, 24, 25
    welding 12-13, 14, 16
computers 6, 7, 16, 17, 25, 28
conveyor belts 14, 18, 20
crankshaft 22, 23
crash tests 8, 28
cylinders 22, 23, 26, 29

design 6-9, 28
    CAD (computer-aided
        design) 7
    prototypes 8, 9, 29
    scale models 7
digital tablet 7, 28
drive train 20, 29

effort 5, 11
electric motors 16

electricity 12, 13
electrodes 12, 13
electrons 13
engine 20, 22-23, 29
exhaust pipe 23, 29

family cars 6
forces 5, 26
forklift trucks 5
fuel 9, 22, 23

hinges 14
hydraulic rams 26, 29
hydrogen gas 23

instrument panel 24, 29

machines 4, 5, 7, 11, 14, 20,
    22, 26

paint storage tanks 18
painting 14, 18-19
pistons 22, 23, 26, 29
prototypes 8, 9, 28
pushes and pulls 5

rack and pinion 20, 21, 29
resistance 13
robots 14-17
    programming 14, 16
    robot arm 16-17, 19, 28
rusting 19

safety 8
scale models 7

sensors 16, 17, 25
spark plugs 22, 23
sports cars 6
spot welding 12, 28
steel 10-11, 19
    cutting 11
steering system 20, 21, 29
suspension 20

three-dimensional (3D)
    pictures 7

valves 22

wedges 11
welding 12-13, 14, 16
    spot welding 12, 28
wheels 20, 21, 26, 29
wind tunnel tests 9, 28
work clothing 18